Silver Lake Quartette

Prohibition bells and songs of the new crusade

For temperance organizations, reform clubs, prohibition camps and

political campaigns

Silver Lake Quartette

Prohibition bells and songs of the new crusade
For temperance organizations, reform clubs, prohibition camps and political campaigns

ISBN/EAN: 9783337265151

Printed in Europe, USA, Canada, Australia, Japan

Cover: Foto ©Andreas Hilbeck / pixelio.de

More available books at **www.hansebooks.com**

PROHIBITION BELLS

— AND —

SONGS OF THE NEW CRUSADE,

— FOR —

Temperance Organizations,

Reform Clubs,

Prohibition Camps,

And Political Campaigns.

COMPILED BY

THE SILVER LAKE QUARTETTE.

1888.

FUNK & WAGNALLS,

18 and 20 Astor Place,   New York.

PRESS OF
FUNK & WAGNALLS,
18 and 20 Astor Place,
NEW YORK

INTO the cause of Prohibition has come with great power the persuasive influence of song. The Silver Lake Temperance Assembly, at Silver Lake, N. Y., has felt it these nine years past, and from that favored place this influence has radiated widely, through the Silver Lake Quartette. In many States, North and South, East and West, during the year just closed, this group of singers has roused vast audiences to enthusiastic approval of Prohibition Party truth.

The songs most popular and effective in their work are given here, with others not less worthy, it is believed, though not yet so enduringly tested by public use. All are fresh ; all were written with direct reference to campaign purposes. Some were prepared in competition for prizes offered by us several months ago, but have undergone searching and repeated trial by the Quartette.

Adaptiveness, not less than musical merit, has been considered an essential quality. Compilers and composers have sought to render PRO-HIBITION BELLS AND SONGS OF THE NEW CRUSADE a thoroughly helpful agency in promoting the growth of aggressive Prohibition sentiment, and its political organization against the saloon. In this effort they have had the active sympathy and assistance of

THE PUBLISHERS.

PROHIBITION BELLS

AND

SONGS OF THE NEW CRUSADE.

No. 1.   **Prohibition Bells.**

Words and Music by SILVER LAKE QUARTETTE.

DUET.

1. The Bells are ring-ing through the land, They sound both loud and clear; They tell to ll the
2. They're ringing out the reign of wrong, They're ringing in the right; Old midnight er-rors
3. They're ringing out the rum-king's doom, He tot-ters on his throne; The right shall win for
4. They're bringing cheer to wom-an's heart, God bless them one and all; Be-fore her faith, and

world a-round, That freedom's day draws near.
flee a-way, Be-hold the dawn-ing light.
God is right—And God shall have His own.
pray'rs and zeal, This gi-ant wrong shall fall.

CHORUS

Hear them Bells! Don't you hear them

Hear them Bells...............

Bells!............ They are ring-ing in the freedom of the land; Hear them

Bells, Bells,

.... Yes, I hear them Bells,

Bells! Prohibition Bells!............ They are ringing in the freedom of the land.

Yes, I hear them Bells,......... ... Pro-hi-bi-tion Bells!

9

No. 2.   When the Glad Day Comes.

Words and Music by SILVER LAKE QUARTETTE.

1. We will shout our loud ho-san-nas, When the glad day comes,
1. Then be read-y for the bat-tle, Till the glad day comes;

We will proudly wave our ban-ners, When the glad day comes:
Nev-er fear the roar and rat-tle, When the glad day comes:

For the wide world will be bet-ter, All man-kind will be our debt-or,
Tho' our foe be so ap-pal-ling, And a-round us men are fall-ing,

If on rum, we forge a fet-ter, When the glad day comes.
Hear the Right's clear bu-gle call-ing, Till the glad day comes.

4

And it comes; Yes, it comes; For behold the skies are clearing, And it

Yes, it comes; Yes, it comes;

comes; Soon we'll hear the mu-sic ringing, From the glad hearts it is

Yes, it comes;

bringing, And the world will join in sing-ing, When the glad day comes.

3 Men of God, the time is nearing,
  When the glad day comes;
Look aloft! the skies are clearing,
  For the glad day comes:
With the word of truth, your token,
Keep your courage all unbroken,
For behold! the Lord hath spoken,
  And the glad day comes.

No. 3.   What I have Seen.

Words by Miss ELLA WHEELER.   Music by EDWARD ROBERTS.

Moderato.

1. I saw a Chris-tian, a
2. I saw his can - di - date
3. I saw a poor drunk-ard
4. I know of a par - ty that's

Tem - per-ance man,   Cast - ing his bal - lot one day at the polls;
sip - ping his beer,   Wip - ing his mus-tashe and lap-ping his jaws; And I
fall in the street;   I saw my Christian man mournful-ly pass, And
form- ing to - day,   Made of the men that are loy - al and brave; They will

One who be - lieves he does what he can,   Toward the re-claim-ing and
said to my-self, "it's de - cid-ed-ly queer, If this is the man that should
mourn-ful - ly say to the sot at his feet, "I have done what I could for such
sweep li-quor tax - es and tariffs a - way, For they nev - er will vote for a

6

What I have Seen.—Concluded.

say - ing of souls. And may be he does— may be he does!
help make our laws!" But may be he is— may be he is!
wrecks, but a - las!" Well, may be he had— may be he had!
drink-ing old knave. You see if they do— see if they do!

I don't say he doesn't. but may be he does! May be, may be,
But I won't say it outright, but may be he is! May be, may be,
I don't say he hadn't, for may be he had! May be, may be,
I don't say I know, but you see if they do! [Omit..............

Slow.

Rit.   *Ending for 4th verse only.*

may be he does!
may be he is!
may be he had!
.....................] You see, you see, you see if they do!

7

No. 4.

Drifting Away.

Mrs. C. L. Schacklock.

D. B. Towner.

Moderato. Tenor or Sop.

1. They are drifting a-way on the sea of life, On its foaming bil-lows tossed:
2. Let the bea-con of hope thro' the darkness shine, For the wand'rers of the wave,
3. They are drifting a-way from the light of home, They are losing manhood's pride,

Alto.

Inst.

They are wea-ry and faint with the fruitless strife, In a moment they'll be lost.
There is mer-cy and love in the Fount di-vine, All the wrecked of earth to save.
They are wrecking their hopes for the life to come, They are drifting with the tide.

Chorus.

drift - ing a - way,.........

Drift - ing a - way,.........

drift-ing a - way,

drift - ing a - way,.........

Drift-ing a - way,

drift-ing a - way,

Drifting Away.—Concluded.

They are drifting farther and far-ther a - way;

They are drifting farther and far-ther a - way; Farther and far-ther a -

drift - ing a - way,

Drift - ing a - way,.......... drifting a - way,

drift - ing a - way,..........

way, Drift-ing a - way, drift-ing a - way,

far - - ther and far - - - ther a - way......

They are drifting, drift - ing farther and farther, farther a-way.

They are drifting far - - ther and far - - - ther a - way, a - way.

They are drift - ing farther and farther a - way......

9

No. 5.

Gambrinus is King.

BASS SOLO.

Words and Music by SILVER LAKE QUARTETTE.

1. Gam - bri - nus is King, he sits on his throne, His scep - tre of
2. He winks and he blinks, and holds up his votes; The Boss - es look
3. "My right I de - mand to gam - ble and bet, I'll pay you a

power he sways o'er his own; His sub - jects are found all
wise, and they all take notes; "The mu - sic I want, a -
part of all that I get; Re - fuse, if you dare, re -

o - ver the land, And they all come down at the King's com - mand.
long with my beer, For part of my votes," he says, with a leer.
mem - ber my frown, Re - pub - li - cans all, you've got to come down."

10

Gambrinus is King.—Concluded.

CHORUS.

And they all come down; Yes, they all come down At his word of com-

Cho. for last Verse. And he shall come down; Yes, he shall come down, Gam - bri - nus, the

mand, They all come down; Oh, they all come down; Yes, they

King, He shall come down; Oh, he shall come down; Yes, he

all come down At his word of command, They all come down.

shall come down At our word of command, He shall come down.

4 "You Bosses who lead, and love your own way,
  You Doctors who preach, you Christians who pray;
  Your party, once grand, shall suffer defeat,
  Unless you come down, *down*, DOWN at my feet."

5 But men who are true to God and the Right,
  Refuse to obey this King in his might;
  His sceptre they'll break, demolish his crown,
  Gambrinus, the King. has got to come down.

11

No. 6. The Saloon Must Go.

Words by J. H. SAMMIS.

Music by EDWARD ROBERTS.

With expression, and not too fast.

1. Friend sa - loon-ist, I'm a - thinkin' Thet thar's got t' be less
2. Nev - er mind a - bout the tax - es, Don't y' wor - ry; when I

drink-in'; Un - cle Sam hes set his min' t' Wipe y'
ax - es Yer ad - vice and yer as - sist - ance Y' kin

out, an' he's a - gwine t'. Pack yer duds, fur "don't cher
an - swer from a dis - tance. Pack yer duds, fur "don't cher

CHORUS.

You must go, You must

know," Friend sa-loon-ist, you must go. That is so;
know," Friend sa-loon-ist, you must go.

The Saloon Must Go.—Concluded.

3 "Prohibition don't prohibit."
That's a fact y' kin exhibit
By and by; but bless my stars, sir,
You will argy through the bars, sir.
Pack yer duds, fur "don't cher know,"
Friend saloonist, you must go.

4 What's all that about yer suin'
Me fur damages accruin'?
Waal, y' may be very knowin',
Allee samee yer a-goin'.
Pack yer duds, fur "don't cher know,"
Friend saloonist, you must go.

5 "See the millions paid in wages?"
See the want, the woe, that rages;
All the waste an' crime an' sinnin',
Fur the dollars thet you're winnin'.
Pack yer duds, fur "dont cher know,"
Friend saloonist, you must go.

6 "Facts an' Figgers!" quit yer lyin';
"Facts an' Figgers!" women sighin';
"Facts an' Figgers!" babes a-cryin';
"Facts an' Figgers!" souls a-dyin';
Pack yer duds, fur "don't cher know,'
Friend saloonist, you must go.

13

No. 7. The Tattered Flag.

Words and Music by Silver Lake Quartette.

Marching movement.

1. Sound the toc - sin, beat the drums, See the Grand Old
2. Grand Old Par - ty! with - out fear, Camp - ing in a

Par - ty comes! Firm of step, ex - ul - tant brave—
grave - yard drear; Out of of - fice, but in luck;

Comes a - gain the land to save! In the grave - yard
Brave of heart and full of pluck; Dig - ging, dig - ging

Slow.

of the past— Lo! an is - sue found at last;
in the ground: Hark! an is - sue has been found!

14

The Tattered Flag.—Concluded.

A tempo.

Let it sound from crag to crag— Glo - ry! found a reb - el flag!
Bend the back—and brave-ly drag From the grave a reb - el flag!

CHORUS.

A flag! a flag! a tat-tered flag; Swell the cho- rus, shout and brag;

Chorus for last verse.
A flag! a flag! so pure and white, Em - blem of e - ter - nal light;

Nev - er since the world was born— Such an is - sue— blow the horn.

Swell the cho- rus, loud and long, Right shall triumph o - ver wrong.

3 Ruined homes and blasted lives;
Hungry children, hopeless wives;
Breaking hearts and weeping eyes;
Dramshops open, manhood dies;
Issues, that the G. O. P.
In its dotage cannot see;
Of the past it proudly brags,—
Lives to fight old rebel flags!

4 Living issues, to the front!
Men to stand the battles' brunt;
Hearts of oak, and nerves of steel,
Men who live, and love, and feel,
This our watch-word, this our cry,
"Liquor traffic, thou must die:"
Till from mountain peak and crag
Waves the Prohibition flag!

15

No. 8. The New Exodus.

"It is vain to say that the Republican party must and shall become a Prohibition party. It must and shall do no such thing. Those who are in it simply to make it so, might as well go at once, for they will not succeed."
—Cin. O. Commercial Gazette. (Rep.)

Words and Music by Silver Lake Quartette.

Not too fast.

1. Lo! the or-der has been heard, In a bit-ter, scorn-ing word, Spread a-
2. There was once a grand-er time, When a pur-pose all sub-lime, Stirred the
3. Now an e-vil day has come, When the friends of Beer and Rum Are en-
4. So we take our fi-nal leave, And we nei-ther cry nor grieve, As we

cresc. *rit.*

broad in all the might of par-ty print; Men of conscience, do you heed? Are you
men who moved the nation with their might; And the par-ty of our choice, Nev-er
treat-ed in the par-ty ranks to stay; And the foes of Rum and Beer Are no
march a-long the roy-al road of Right; Tho' at first we may be few, Soon with-

The New Exodus.—Concluded,

a tempo.

cra-ven grown, indeed? Then a - rise in right-eous wrath and take the hint!
by un-friend-ly voice, Spoke to those who bore the ban - ner of the Right.
longer want-ed here, But have spe-cial word "*at once*" to go their way.
in our par - ty new, There'll be mill-ions march-ing on - ward in their might.

CHORUS.
Animated.

We will go, we will go, From the grand old

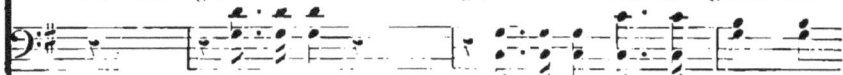

We will go, we will go,

par - ty we will go; With our bag - gage in our hand, We'll o -

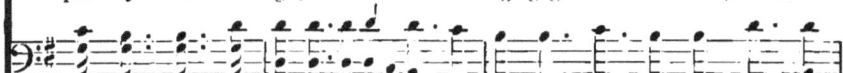

we will go;

bey the wise command, And marching on to vic - to - ry we'll go.

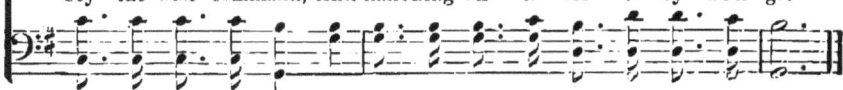

17

No. 9.   Prohibition Prize Song.

Words by Hannah A. Foster.

Music by Edward Roberts.

1. List - en! 'tis the roll - call drum, — Clear the track! they
2. We've a li - cense foe to fight, Tax - ing wrong can't

come, they come! Men of might whom du - ty claims, Men who
make it right! Laws for reg - u - lat - ing sin In this

an - swer to their names; Men of con - science, brain and pluck,
con - flict can - not win. On! nor heed the roar and smoke,

Charge! the sig - nal hour has struck; Ou - ward, with the vic - tor's shout,
Smite him where he'll feel the stroke! Smite the spoil - er with a will,

Prohibition Prize Song.—Concluded.

3 Hark! what means this rush and noise?
"Tis the coming of the boys!
Give them place, ye veteran bands—
See the ballots in their hands!
Open ranks, and cheer them in,
They have come to fight and win,
This their countersign to-day:
"Voting as our mothers pray."

4 Let the poor old parties try
License low, and license high,
Tell the years that must be spent
Making public sentiment!
Are we slaves—or are we men?
Out upon the traffic, then!
Fearless—since our cause is just;
Victors—for in God we trust!

* While Soprano sings first two lines of the Chorus, the other voices will sing the word "Rally" softly, at first, and increase in power.

19

No. 10.   Cranks.

Words and Music by SILVER LAKE QUARTETTE.

1. We be-long to the ar-my of cranks, And we owe some good fel-
2. If you think that a crank is N. G., Please re-mem-ber how oft-
3. We shall turn the old par-ties both out, Ere our la-bors are end-

low our thanks, For a name that be-fits us pre-cise-ly; We
en you see Might-y force from so fee-ble in-ven-tion. No
ed, no doubt,—And there's noth-ing some crank should do quicker; The

mean for mankind. a good turn, As all in due sea-son will learn, For
pow-er counts much till applied, And cranks, it is nev-er de-nied, Have
pros-pect may make them both sad, But o-ver it we are so glad, That

CHORUS.

cranks a good turn do so nice-ly. Oh, he is a crank, ha, ha, And
u-ses too man-y to men-tion.
oft-en, while singing, we snick-er.

20

Cranks.—Concluded.

he is a crank, ho, ho ; We are all of us cranks, Won't you come to our ranks, And

laugh as we mer - ri - ly go? Oh! Ha, ha, ha, Ha,

ha, ha, Ha, ha, ha, Ha, ha, ha, Ha, ha, ha, Ha, ha, ha, Ha!

4 From our course we shall ne'er turn aside,
  Though the world may assail or deride,
But go on with our grand revolution;
  For cranks must keep turning, to go,
  And we are so cranky, you know,
We give each good turn restitution. —CHORUS.

5 We shall turn the world right, by and by;
  And it's better to laugh than to cry
At the sneers of the men who defame us;
  Some day, when our mission is done,
  They'll claim the reward we have won,
And brag of it more than they blame us. —CHORUS.

No. 11. Prohibition Chariot.

Words by N. Allen Lindsay. Music by Silver Lake Quartette.

1. We are marshalled for the fight, we are ea - ger for the
2. See the maj - es - ty and might, as it grand - ly rolls a -

fray, When the trum - pet calls "to arms!" we are
long; In its path is morn - ing light, and its

read - y to o - bey; For the char - i - ot of truth is a -
wheels are joy and song; 'Tis a glo - ry to the right, but a

roll - ing on its way, And right is bound to win.
ter - ror to the wrong, And right is bound to win.

Prohibition Chariot.—Concluded.

Chorus.

And we'll roll, roll the char-i-ot a-long; And we'll

roll, roll the char-i-ot a-long; And we'll roll, roll the

char-i-ot a-long, For right is bound to win.

3 Roll the chariot along, there is nothing can oppose,
   For it breaks oppression down and all evil overthrows;
   Soon the desert shall rejoice, and shall blossom like the rose,
     For right is bound to win.

4 Then forward in its track, for the battle has begun,
   Not an effort must we slack till our earthly work is done;
   We shall hurl their legions back, and shall keep what we have won,
     For right is bound to win.

No. 12. The Only Way.

Words by EDWARD CARSWELL.

Music by DAVENPORT KERRISON.

1. Do you
2. Mor - al
3. The question's

mf

hear the bells a - ring - ing, Re-sound-ing far and near?—
sua - sion we have tried, To fight the li - quor fiend; But
one of life or death, Not how much shall he pay; Not

Some on - ly soft - ly, gent - ly toll - ing, Oth - ers loud and
found the foe im - preg - na - ble, By law and li - cense
li - cense high or li - cense low, But shall he go or

21

The Only Way.—Continued.

clear;
screened;
stay!

Yes, some as chil-dren sob-bing sound, While oth-ers
No pit-y moved his sto-ny heart, He scoffed at
Can dol-lars pay for brok-en hearts? Or save the

seem to scream;
pray'rs and tears—
souls that die?

But tell me, why the ring-ing, pray, And
But now he trem-bles in his fort, When
If not, there's but one thing to do, And

Chorus.

what the ring-ers mean?
from a-far he hears—
this must be our cry—

Waltz time.

P. R. O.

The Only Way.—Concluded.

H. I. B.— Hold on— that's it— now I see!

Pró - hib - it — Pro - hib - it -- P. R. O. H. I. B. I. T.

No. 13. De Jub'lee Bells.

Words by A. J. MORRIS.

Music by EDWARD ROBERTS.

1. Oh! Darkies, don't you hear de sound, Dat troo de pine tree's sing-in'!
2. It   am   a sound we all should love, So much like an - gels' voic - es,
3. De white folks dey has got stirred up To save dere homes and chil-lun,
4. And when we git de dram-shop out, Our nay - bors all get so - ber,

26

De Jub'lee Bells.--Concluded.

And murm'ring down de ribber's bed, Like sweet-toned bells a-ring-in'?
And speaks re-demp-tion to our race From whiskey's aw-ful curs-es.
Dey ought to done dis long be-fo, We all should be right wil-lin.
We den will raise a mi-ty shoat, And spend our days in clo-ver.

CHORUS.

Oh! ring de bells, de jub'-lee bells,
Yes, ring de bells, de jub'-lee bells, An'
set dere tungs a-clang-in', For Pro-hi-bi-tion soon will
come; yes, t'will come, An' whis-key get a-bang-in'!

27

No. 14.

A Temperance Dodger.

Words and Music by SILVER LAKE QUARTETTE.

1. Oh, I'm a Temp'rance Dodger, Would you like to know my name?
2. Yes, I'm a Temp'rance Dodger, The sa-loon I think a sin,

But I think I'll let you guess it, If to you it's all the same.
And I pray a-gainst it oft-en With an unc-tion that should win.

My de-light is Pro-hi-bi-tion, On the street and in the church,
I be-lieve in Pro-hi-bi-tion, When to God I make ap-peal,

'Tis on-ly at the bal-lot box I leave it in the lurch.
'Tis on-ly at the bal-lot box My faith I do con-ceal.

28

A Temperance Dodger.—Concluded.

Yes, in-deed, { I am } { he is } a Dodg-er, We ad-mit that it is true;

Yes, in-deed, { I am } { he is } a Dodg-er, Just the same as some of you.

{ My } { His } de-light is Pro-hi-bi-tion, On the street and in the church,

But standing at the bal-lot box { I } { You } leave it in the lurch.

3 Oh, I'm a Temp'rance Dodger,
  The saloon I think a crime,
But he is a mad fanatic
  Who condemns it all the time.
So I stand for Prohibition,
  On the street and in the church,
'Tis only at the ballot box
  I leave it in the lurch.

4 Oh, I'm a Temp'rance Dodger,
  There's my wife a worker, true,
In the ranks of noble women,
  Known as W. C. T. U.
I will help her all I can, sir,
  In the church and on the street,
'Tis only at the ballot box
  I aid in her defeat.

29

No. 15. The Middle of the King's Highway.

Words and Music by SILVER LAKE QUARTETTE.

1. We've en-tered in this fight, For God, and Home, and Right, And
2. The two old par-ties, long, We've begged with prayer and song, But
3. The Dem-o-crats say Rum, Re-pub-li-cans say 'Um,' And

with the help of God we mean to stay; We now pro-pose to stand, With
from our plea they both have turned a-way; Now as they take no heed, We
with our prin-ci-ples they try to play; We bid them both a-dieu, With

bal-lots in our hand, And keep a-long the middle of the King's high-way.
straightway are a-greed To keep a-long the middle of the King's high-way.
hon-est men and true, We'll keep a-long the middle of the King's high-way.

CHORUS, by J. M. WHYTE, by permission.

Just keep a-long the mid-dle of the
Just keep a-long the mid-dle of the King's high-way, Just

The Middle of the King's Highway.—Concluded.

King's high - - way, Just keep a -

keep a - long the mid-dle of the King's high-way; Don't you turn to the

long the middle of the King's high - - way Just

right of the King's highway; Don't you turn to the left of the King's highway, But

keep a - long the mid-dle of the King's

keep a - long the mid-dle, just keep a-long the middle, just keep a-long the

high - - way.

mid-dle of the King's highway.

4 They call us cranks and fools,
Because we won't be tools
To help them into offices that pay;
But whether fools or cranks,
We say "Good Bye" with thanks,
And keep along the middle of the King's
highway.

31

No. 16. The March of Prohibition.

Words by R. L. Bruce. Music by Edward Roberts.

Not too fast.

1. In a hov-el dark and drear, bends a moth-er pale with fear,
2. In a breath-ing hole of hell, where ac-curs-ed vi-pers dwell,

O'er her chil-dren cold and rag-ged on the floor; For the
Sits a bloat-ed wreck of what was once a man; And be-

rum-fiend's curs-ed blight all her day has turned to night,
fore his blood-shot eyes, hor-rid de-mons seem to rise,

Slow and impressive.

And the wolf with hun-gry maw is at the door.
Hiss and crawl and screech as on-ly de-mons can.

✻ Small notes for Organ. All voices sing the Soprano here.

The March of Prohibition.—Concluded.

Tramp, tramp, tramp, she hears star - va - tion, sees his face so gaunt and
Tramp, tramp, tramp, the aw - ful le - gions from the land of mid- night

white; God of Mer - cy, hear her cry, ris - ing to thy
gloom, To his ter - ror - gleam - ing eyes, seem in ser - ried

throne on high, Stir the hearts of men to bat - tle for the right.
ranks to rise, While be - fore him yawns e - ter - nal hope - less doom.

3 In a bright and cheery place, full of dig-
  nity and grace,
  Noble women gather battling for the
  right;
Take the drunkard by the hand; give him
  courage, help him stand;
  Lead him upward, cheer him onward
  into light.
Chorus.
Tramp, tramp, tramp, the saved are
  marching; hearts are light and hopes
  are strong,
And there's joy in earth and heaven, o'er
  the wanderer forgiven.
And the home is full of light and love
  and song.

4 But, alas! the fatal snare dashes hope
  and baffles prayer,
  And the saved are daily falling 'neath
  its power;
Rise ye men of heart and sense, drive the
  cursèd monster hence,
  Prohibition be our watchword from this
  hour.
Chorus.
Tramp, tramp, tramp, we give no
  quarter, marching on the lost to
  save,
Satan's minions we defy, Prohibition
  is our cry,
And we'll shout it over rum's dis-
  'honored grave.

33

No. 17.   Grand Old Cause of Right.

Words and Music by Silver Lake Quartette.

BASS SOLO.

1. There's a grand old cause, and we call it Right, 'Tis gird - ed by truth and love;
2. 'Tis a grand old cause that shall guard the boy From the wine - cup's temp-ting snare,
3. For this grand old cause we will work and pray, For Right shall our votes be cast,

It was sent to earth by the Lord of might, From His great white throne a - bove.
And the mother's heart shall be filled with joy, As she breathes the even - ing pray'r.
And this grand old cause with re - sist - less sway Shall con - quer the wrong at last.

CHORUS.

Oh, grand old cause of Right, For thy suc - cess we pray; With

ho - ly might and bless - ed light, Speed on, speed on thy way.

34

No. 18.

Shout! Shout! Shout!

Words and Music by SILVER LAKE QUARTETTE.

1. Hear the mill-ions march-ing forth, Of the South and of the North, To the
2. Sore the griev-ing and the tears, Long the wait-ing of the years, While the
3. Out of per-il and of pain, Will our God the glo-ry gain, For His

bat-tle of the Right a-gainst the Wrong; Loy-al age and gal-lant youth, Bearing
souls of men grow stronger for the fray; Now we see the dawn sublime, Of a
faith-ful who de-fend the cause of Right; Er-ror trembles on its throne, Truth to

on the flag of truth, As they thun-der to the skies their bat-tle song.
glad-der, grand-er time, As we join the march-ing mill-ions on their way.
tri-umph now is grown, And the world will see the splen-dors of its might.

CHORUS.

Shout! shout! shout! the Lord is mighty, On we march at His command; To the glo-ry of His

ritard.

name, We will smite the monster shame, For the sake of God, and Home and Native Land.

Copyright, 1887, by C. H. MEAD

35

No. 19.

The Clarion Call.

Words by JAMES L. ELDERDICE.   Music by SILVER LAKE QUARTETTE.

1. Brave men of blue, brave men of gray, God's clar-ion calls to arms to-day; From East and West, from South and North, The ea-ger hosts are march-ing forth. Who once were foes are breth-ren now, And all have pledged the sol-emn vow, To

2. The hosts of God know not de-feat, His clar-ion nev-er sounds re-treat; With heav'ns ar-til-lery at com-mand, What foe our on-slaught can with-stand? The cry goes up from sea to sea, "Our rum-curs'd coun-try shall be free!" Oh!

3. Some time in le-gends and in lays, Of the on-com-ing, hap-pier days, The sons of blue and gray shall tell, How once were li-censed paths to hell; How once the land with crimes was red, And wives and chil-dren starved for bread; How

36

The Clarion Call.—Concluded.

rest not till they o - ver- throw Our common coun-try's dead - liest foe.
hark the might-y shout that comes, "Our God, our coun - try and our homes."
once *our* hosts the fight did wage, That ushered in *their* gold - en age.

CHORUS.

For - ward, then, ... brave vol - un - teers, The clar - ion

For - ward, then,

call .... is in our ears; Lift the glo - - rious standard

The clarion call is in our ears; Lift the glorious standard

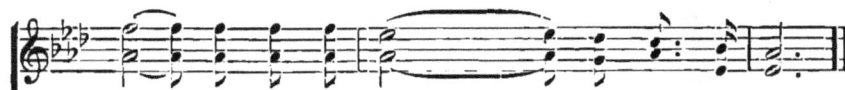

high, And on-ward press .... to vic - to - ry!

high, And on - ward press to vic - to - ry!

No. 20.   Tweedle Dee and Tweedle Dum.

Words and Music by SILVER LAKE QUARTETTE.

1. Two old par - ties, see! they come: Twee - dle Dee and
2. Both are glad, and both are glum: Twee - dle Dee and
3. Both can talk, and both be mum: Twee - dle Dee and

Twee - dle Dum; They both are old, de - crep - it and worn, For
Twee - dle Dum; For civ - il ser - vice they both a - dore, And
Twee - dle Dum; They both are for tar - iff, high or low, They

years have passed, since ei - ther was born; But still they live by
civ - il ser - vice they both ab - hor; 'Tis of - fice they want, and
both des - pise the mormons, you know; Be - cause they a - gree, they

ta - king a horn Of beer, or Ja - mai - ca Rum. ⎫
noth - ing more, Ex - cept - ing the Beer and Rum. ⎬ Oh!
fight and blow, And nev - er leave out the Rum. ⎭

38

Tweedle Dee and Tweedle Dum.—Concluded.

CHORUS.

Yes, they are Twee - dles, Yum, Yum, Yum, One is
Dee and the oth - er is Dum; But the puz - zling thing, as
all can see, Is to pick out Dum from Twee - dle Dee.

4 From the same old stock they come:
   Tweedle Dee and Tweedle Dum;
   They both are honest, up to their eyes,
   And all things honest they both despise,
   While each can tell you the others' size,
   And also the price of Rum.

5 But, at last, their time has come:
   Tweedle Dee and Tweedle Dum;
   For Dee says Dum is a rascal true,
   And Dum says Dee is a rascal too;
   They both are right, so the thing we'll do—
   Is bounce them both and their Rum.

No. 21.

Republicans and Democrats.

Words and Music by SILVER LAKE QUARTETTE.

DUET.

1. There is a stir throughout the land, / A lot of cranks, oh! what a band! } Re-publicans and Demo - crats;
2. You had the power, long years a - go, / To stop this tide of crime and woe, } Re-publicans and Demo - crats;
3. In Eighty-Four, with-out ex - cuse, / You heaped on us un-told a - buse, } Re-pub-li-cans, Re-publi - cans;

Fa - nat-ics, fools, and cra - zy, too, Their numbers are no lon-ger few;
But to this cause you've been un-true, When now, too late, a - las! you'll rue;
In ef - fi - gy you hung St. John, And then you tried to scowl us down;

Pray tell us, sirs, what you will do, Re - pub - licans and Dem-o - crats?
Oh dear, oh dear, what will you do, Re - pub - licans and Dem-o - crats?
But don't you see, we're still in town, Re - pub - licans, Re-pub - li - cans?

4 Is there within this hall to-night,
   A Democrat, a Democrat;
Who never yet has voted right,
   A Democrat, a Democrat;
Now what's the use, pray, don't you see,
Your poor old party is N. G.?
'Tis soaked in Rum, and so 'twill be.
   Oh Democrat, poor Democrat.

5 There is a party, bless the Lord,
   Republicans and Democrats;
With Prohibition, its watchword,
   Republicans and Democrats;
Come, swell our ranks, and join our band,
And then, with ballots in our hand,
We'll vote for Home and Native Land
   Republicans and Democrats.

Copyright, 1887, by C. H. Mead.

40

No. 22.

We'll be There.

Southern Melody.   Words and arrangement by SILVER LAKE QUARTETTE.

1. We stand for home, we stand for truth,
2. We're bound to put this rum-fiend out,
3. We stand un-moved by jibe or jeer,

When e-lec-tion day comes round we'll be there;

We stand for age, we stand for youth;
And when 'tis done we'll raise a shout,
No par-ty whip can make us fear,

When e-lec-tion-day comes round we'll be there.

CHORUS.

I'll be there, I'll be there, When e-lec-tion-day comes round we'll all be there.

I'll be there,

4 The two old parties we may kill,
When election-day comes round we'll be there;
But then we all will be here still,
When election-day comes round we'll be there.
Cho.—I'll be there, etc.

5 You'd best come in and join our band,
When election-day comes round we'll be there;
And vote for Home and Native Land,
When election-day comes round we'll be there.
Cho.—I'll be there, etc.

No. 23.   The Coming Hero.

Words by DWIGHT WILLIAMS.   Music by SILVER LAKE QUARTETTE.

1. He comes, the he - ro, on his way, With loy - al hosts at -
2. We'll go to Wash - ing - ton some day, And hail him there with

tend - ing; For him the mil - lions fond - ly pray, At
ban - ners! And Boys in Blue and Boys in Gray Will

low - ly al - tars bend - ing; Get read - y for the
join the glad ho - san - nas; We come from South and

cham - pi - on! The line of march is quick - er; Swing,
North a - like, With loy - al hearts u - nit - ed, And

The Coming Hero.—Concluded.

swing your ban - ners in the sun! The bat - tle ranks are thick-er.
for our com - mon cause we strike, To freedom on - ly plighted.

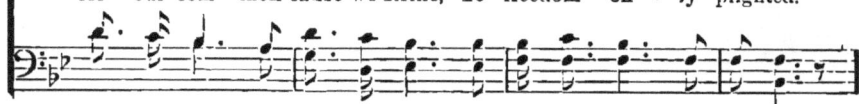

CHORUS.

A Pro - hi - bi - tion Pres - i - dent Is com-ing, boys, get read - y!

Vote in, vote in the grand e - vent, With columns strong and stead- y.

3 Hark! 'tis the people's battle cry,
  With loyal words and hearty,
And written on their banner high
  "The Prohibition Party!"
From "Third" to "First" we'll push our way,
  The battle is before us;
We'll sing in Washington some day
  A grander Union chorus.

43

No. 24.　　Old Rummie's Going Away.

Words by J. A. McMillan.　　　　　　　　　　　Music by Wm. Clark.

TENOR SOLO.

1. Say, neighbors, have you seen Old Rum-mie,　With a scowl upon his face?
2. He swears blue streaks about this coun-try,　And he's aw-ful mad, I fear;
3. I　tell you, friends, 'twill just be glo-rious　For　to see Old Rummie go!

Ha! ha! ha!　I　met him on　the street this morn-ing,
But all　the same, he's go-ing to tra - vel
We'll feel as though we'd all　em - i - grat-ed

BASS SOLO.

1st verse. No! no! no!
Other verses. Oh! oh! oh!

And he's go - ing　to leave the place.
With his whis - key,　wine and beer.
To a　lit - tle　heav'n be-low.

He is go - ing　to leave the place.
With his whis - key, wine and beer.
To　a　lit - tle heav'n be - low.

He sees　the dark clouds o'er him gath-er,　And he fears the com-ing storm;
He knows we hate　his curs - ed business, For he hears the chil-dren cry;
Our dar - ling chil - dren shall be　hap - py, And free from the drunkard's snare;

4-1

Old Rummie's Going Away.—Continued,

So he thinks he'd better pack his bag-gage, For it's getting mighty warm.
He says we fools don't know any bet-ter Than to go and vote it "dry."
When "a school on ev-ery hill-top's plan-ted, And saloons are found nowhere!"

Yes, it's get - ting might - y warm.
Yes, we're sure to vote it "dry."
And sa - loons are found no - where!

Is it get - ting might - y warm?
We are sure to vote it "dry."
And sa - loons are found no-where!

CHORUS.

Old Rummie's go - ing a - way, And the

a - way,

coun - try shall be free; So,

Yes, the coun - try shall be free;

45

Old Rummie's Going Away.—Concluded.

neighbors, come and join in the cho-rus, And we'll shout the ju - bi-

lee,.............. And we'll shout the ju - bi - lee.

And we'll shout the ju - bi - lee.

4 When Rummie's gone we'll all shout
    And we'll have a jolly time;   ["glory!"]
The rich and poor will both have plenty,
    And we'll bid good-by to crime.
Policemen will be scarcely needed,
    And the tramp shall be no more;
We'll turn the jail to a cotton factory
    And the poor-house to a store.

5 We're going now to cast our ballots,
    And we'll vote just as we pray;
So the saloon will be snowed under,
    For 't will be a cold, cold day.
Oh, then we'll say good-by to Rummie,
    As he takes his long, long walk!
Of course he hates to start on his journey;
    But it is no use to talk.

No. 25.   The Charge.

Words by Curtis May.   Music by J. Mervin Hull.

1. Men who won the bat - tles Fought in years gone by! Men who bore the
2. Hear the cry of childhood Bowed with bit - ter woe, See the wife fall,

46

The Charge.—Concluded.

ban - ner, Sworn to do or die! Do you sit in qui - et?
strick-en By a drunk-en blow. Now an ev - il threat-ens,

Do you shrink or fear? Up! the country calls you, Up! the foe is here.
Scorching to the soul Would you know its na-ture? Seek it in the bowl.

CHORUS.

Do you sit in qui - et? Do you shrink or fear?

a tempo.

Up! the coun - try calls you, Up! the foe is here.

3 Hear the charge we bring you,
   You who act for all!
Meet the need that beckons,
   Though the bravest fall.
Strike the evil crouching
   At the nation's heart:
Who dares not be loyal
   Let him stand apart!

4 By the child that prattles
   On your knee to-night;
By the wife whose smiling
   Fills your house with light;
By the tender mother
   Who bent over you;
We who can but charge you,
   Charge you to be true.

47

No. 26.

Cheers for the Veteran.

Dedicated to NEAL DOW, September 28, 1887.

Words and Music by SILVER LAKE QUARTETTE.

1. Cheers for the Vet - er - an, comrades, Well has our trib - ute been
2. Ech - o them hills of New Eng - land; Hear them, wide plains of the

won; Long has he fought, for the good we have sought; Dar-ing the
West; Swell the glad song, as we send it a - long, All who love

deeds he has done! Bring him the crown of the vic - tor,
man - hood the best; Greet - ings and hon - or to conscience,

Wreathe it with gar - lands a - round; Tears for the dead, who for -
Scep - tered, o - beyed, on its throne; Glo - ry's rich gain, for the

Cheers for the Veteran.—Concluded.

ev - er have fled, Cheers for the liv - ing love - crowned.
he - ro from Maine, Ev - ery-where man-hood is known.

Chorus.

Cheers for the vet - er - an com-rades, Fling glo-ry's gar-lands a - round;

Tears for the dead, who for-ev-er have fled, Cheers for the living love crowned.

3 Peace to the Veteran, comrades,
  Nearing the sunset at last;
Long through the day, has he fought by
    the way;
Eastward his shadows are cast,
Sweet be his rest, when at evening,
  Softly the night falleth down,
Glad the "Well done," of the masterful
  Bringing his radiant crown.   [One.

4 Cheers for the Veteran, comrades,
  Daring the deeds he has done,
Still as they pray, must men fight in the
    fray,
Just is the battle begun;
On to the front, in the conflict,
  We with fresh courage will go;
God in His might, leading ever the fight,
  Never defeat shall we know.

No. 27. We're not so Lonesome as we Used to be.

Words and Music by Silver Lake Quartette.

1. Look around, brethren! tell us what you see, Thousands are ris - ing for the
2. Look around, brethren! tell us what you hear, Pray'rs of the peo - ple for suc -

Right; We're not so lonesome as we used to be, We're
cess; While God bends o - ver with His list'n - ing ear, And

grand - ly gathering might. Li - quor men tremble, fear - ing sud-den fall;
waits our cause to bless. Li - quor men cursing, threat-en us and rave;

Pol - i - ti - cians mar - vel iu a - maze; We're dig-ging for them
Pol - i - ti - cians won - der and up - braid; But curs - ing can - not

We're not so Lonesome.—Concluded.

all now, a grave that is not small, We'll bu - ry them one of these days!
save from the Traffic's o - pen grave, Where all of its friends shall be laid.

CHORUS.

No! we're not so lonesome as we used to be, Thousands are ris-ing for the

Right; From the ham - lets of the val - ley, from the cit - ies by the

sea, We're gath'ring Victory's might.

3 Look around, brethren! tell us what you
    feel,
  Prohibition's bound to win;
The bells of victory, with peal on peal,
  To ring will soon begin.
Liquor's reign ended, Law shall be obeyed,
  Politicians make it their delight;
Prosperity shall come, as we bid adieu to
    Rum,
  Then rally with conquering might.

51

No. 28   Recruiting Song.

Words by I. C. JOHNSON.

Music by SILVER LAKE QUARTETTE.

1. We're re-cruiting up an ar-my for the cause, That will pu-ri-fy and
2. For King Al-co-hol is stubborn, and he's strong, And there's few to lead the

ex-e-cute the laws; We are marching and we're drumming, And the
Temp'rance hosts a-long: For the Dem-o-crats are naughty, And Re-

pat-ri-ots are com-ing, And the wel-kin is a-ringing with ap-plause.
pub-li-cans are haughty, And they'll nev-er join the bat-tle 'gainst the wrong.

3

We are drilling up the soldiers for the war,
For we sniff the mighty battle from afar;
  We are growing brave and steady,
  And our martial tramp already
Has alarmed the whiskey tyrant by the jar.

4

We are building up a party for the right,
And the hope of speedy victory is bright;
  For we're *doing* what we're *saying*,
  And we're *voting* as we're *praying*,
And in principle and conscience there is might.

5

We are hurting other parties, so they say;
'Cause they can't afford to give the right of way.
  So Republicans are howling,
  And the Democrats are growling,
But we're marching right along to gain the day.

6

Lay aside your vain and hopeless party pranks,
Come along and join the Prohibition ranks,
  And we'll get so mighty frisky,
  That we'll overturn the whiskey,
For we're all a mighty jolly set of cranks.

No. 29. The Temperance Call.

Words by JENNIE C. YOUNG.   Music by F. J. FULLER.

Moderato.

1. Throughout the land, On ev - ery hand, An earn - est call is heard;
2. It gath - ers force, From ev - ery source, From age and sun - ny youth;
3. O Thou, to whom We all may come, With ev - ery joy and grief.

It rolls a - long, Each day more strong, Till ev - ery heart is stirred.
Be - fore its pow'r, The de-mons cow'r, As false-hood shrinks from truth.
Hear Thou our cry, Lord, save, we die, Oh, come and bring re - lief.

From far and near The call we hear, From cit - y, town and wood,
This call we hear, Oh shall we fear The ty - rant bold and strong?
Then on we'll go Till all shall know That Thou hast heard our call;

And proud heads bend, While pray'rs as-cend To the au - thor of all good.
Our Fa - ther's hand Shall guide our band To vic - t'ry o'er the wrong.
Till ev - ery knee Shall bow to Thee, And crown Him Lord of all.

No. 30.   It's Got to Go!

Words and Music by SILVER LAKE QUARTETTE.

SOLO.

QUARTETTE.

1. { The li - quor traf - fic in our land, Has got to go! yes,
   { For we're a bold, de - ter-m'ned band, It's got to go! yes,
2. { Bar - keep-ers, with their a - prons white, Have got to go! yes,
   { Be - cause their bu - siness is not right, They've got to go! yes,

DUETT.

got to go! } We've pledged our word and will not fear To
got to go! }
got to go! } We think it time they heard a noise; Too
got to go! }

fight the band - ed hosts of Beer, And though the Rum - mies
long they've robbed us of our boys, And shad - owed home with

QUARTETTE.

think it queer, It's got to go! Yes, got to go!
all its joys; They've got to go! Yes, got to go!

It's Got to Go!—Concluded.

3 The politicians, grinning 'round,
  Have got to go! yes, got to go!
For on this question they're unsound,
  And they must go! yes, they must go!
To rant and rage will not avail,
Nor us with curses to assail;
Our cause is right, and shall not fail,
  So they must go! yes, they must go!

4 The two old parties, breeding hate,
  Have got to go! yes, got to go!
For us they need no longer wait,
  But "go at once," forever go!

Too low before King Alcohol
They cringe in fear, and meekly fall;
We have no use for them at all,
  They've got to go! yes, got to go!

5 Come, brothers, lift a mighty shout,
  "It's got to go! it's got to go!
We'll drive the Liquor Traffic out,—
  It's got to go! yes, got to go!"
When from this curse our land is free,
A prospered people we shall be;
Till then we'll sing from sea to sea,
  "It's got to go! it's got to go!"

No. 31.   Prohibition Party.

S. S. M.   MALE VOICES.   Music by SILVER LAKE QUARTETTE.

1. One good-ly morn a babe was born, A youngster hale and heart-y;
2. A man from Maine, in touching strain, With loft-y pa-thos ranking,

His spon-sors came, and gave him name, 'Twas "Prohi-bi-tion Par-ty."
Was heard to sigh: "Dear Brother Frye, That ba-by needs a spanking."

Prohibition Party.—Concluded.

The ba - by grew, as scarce they do, It made the "Boss-es" shiv-er;
But ere th'old man could work his plan, And do the shin-gle act, sir,

Un - til, you see, the G. O. P. Dream'd bad-ly of "Salt Riv-er."
The doughty youth did vote, forsooth, A well-grown man, in fact, sir.

CHORUS.

Then shout with glee, ye brave and free, In cho - rus full and heart-y

For coming days shall hail with praise The Pro-hi - bi - tion Par - ty.

No. 32. The Prohibition Battle Song.

Words by F. O. Thurber. Music by T. F. Fuller.

BARITONE SOLO, or Unison Voices.

1. A - rise! ye Pro - hi - bi - tion hosts, and act ye well your parts;

INST.

Let "Vig - i - lance" your watchword be. A mil - lion ach - ing hearts

Are call - ing us in pleading tones from val - ley, hill and plain,

The Prohibition Battle Song. — Continued.

En - treat - ing us to nev - er rest   till al - co - hol is slain.

CHORUS. — Unison.

Then sound a - loud the bu - gle call, the de - mon Rum must die!

"Our God and home and na - tive land," shall be   our bat - tle cry;

Unison.

Our hosts will num - ber mil - lions yet, of stur - dy men and true,

58

The Prohibition Battle Song.--Concluded.

And Al - co - hol shall die the death in Eight-een Nine - ty-two.

2.

We do not come with leaden ball, nor sword of tempered steel,
Nor yet with grape and cannister, nor tramp of iron heel,
Unless the foe should challenge us to battle for the right:
Then every man will quickly seek the thickest of the fight.

3.

We come with eyes in faith upraised to Him in whom we trust;
With hearts undaunted, for we know our cause is right and just.
No matter what the odds may be, we boldly take our stand,
And vote for Prohibitionists to rule our native land.

4.

Each city, town and farmer's cot in all the country wide,
Is pouring forth its noblest sons to join the swelling tide.
We're growing stronger every day, in men who dare to do,
Who always vote as they have prayed, and dare to own it, too.

5.

And so we march triumphant on, with firm and steady tread;
We neither turn to right nor left, but journey straight ahead.
The time is past for backward steps in pathways we have trod;
We'll do our part with all our might, and leave the rest with God.

No. 33.   Sing, ye Freemen.

Words by A. J. MORRIS.   Music by SILVER LAKE QUARTETTE.

1. Hark! a voice of might-y im-port Comes with ev-ery
2. Long the curs-ed chain has held us, Bind-ing mil-lions

breeze a-long; It is ech-oed from the hill-sides,
in its clasp, But we soon shall see de-liv-'rance,

And the val-leys swell the song. From the East and
Light is dawn-ing; yes, at last. See the ser-ried

West it gath-ers, North and South take up the strain,
ranks of foe-men Quail be-fore our ban-ner bright,

Sing, ye Freemen.—Concluded.

"Pro - hi - bi - tion" is the watchword, And the vic - t'ry
For up - on it is em - bla - zoned "Pro - hi - bi - tion,"

CHORUS.

we will gain. Sing the ju - bi - lee, ye free - men,
true and right.

Chris - tians, vote as now ye pray; Li - quor's chains shall

soon be bro - ken, Hail! O hail the glo - rious day!

3 Rally then, ye freemen mighty,
  Trust in God, who shields the right;
Forward, march, the foe to conquer,
  Get ye ready for the fight!

With our armor burnished brightly,
  Weapons held by hands so true,
Save our country from her danger,
  Fail her not, she trusts to you.

No. 34. Keep your Ballots White.

Words by MARGARET E. STEWART. Music by SILVER LAKE QUARTETTE.

1. On - ward, men of faith and cour - age, Leg - is - late to - day;
2. On - ward, men of zeal and ac - tion, Swell the ranks of war;

Stand for God, and home, and coun - try; Vote, and fight, and pray.
Hold the stand - ard strong and stead - y, Gath -'ring near and far.

E - vil shall not al - ways con - quer, Heav - en speeds the right;
Strike where God and man-hood call you; Strike a - gainst the wrong!

Slow.

Keep your cour - age strong and stead - y, Keep your bal - lots white.
Strike, and cut the chains a - sun - der That have bound the strong!

Keep your Ballots White.—Concluded.

In our bat - - - tle for the Right, Let us

Chorus.

In our bat - tle for the Right, for the Right,

ral - - ly all our might; We shall win,........

Let us ral - ly all our might, all our might; We shall

.... for God is lead-ing,

Ritard.

win, for God is leading, God is lea l-ing, Keep your ballots white.

3 Onward, men of truth and conscience,
   There is work for you;
   Danger calls, and can you linger
   While your hearts are true?
   Let your hearts be hot for justice,
   Scorn to compromise,
   Waver not, for heaven wills it,
   Truth at last shall rise.

No. 35.

Protection.

Words and Music by Silver Lake Quartette.

1. The Grand Old Par-ty was in a sad plight, In search of
2. Pro - tec - tion for what? For cop-per and steel; Pro-tec - tion for

some - thing for which it could fight; But a - las! its searching was
wool, for beef and for veal; Pro - - tec - tion for yarn, for

all . in vain, Un - til it had heard from a man named Blaine.
dry-goods and toys; Pro - tec - tion for mules, but none for the boys.

CHORUS.

Just list-en to Blaine! Ex - act - ly ! "Pro-tec-tion!" So
What ! Blaine of Maine?

61.

Protection.—Concluded.

runs his re-frain; It is plain that Blaine, so gay and heart-y, Is a-
fraid free trade will ru-in his par-ty; 'Tis plain to Blaine that
tax on whis-key, Pro-tec-tion will yield from trouble so ris-ky.

3.
Protection for tin, for hairpins and wax;
Protection for iron, for toothpicks and tacks;
Protection for gum, for brushes and combs;
Protection for lace, but none for the homes.

4.
Protection for sheep, for dogs and for cows;
Protection for zinc, for paper and plows;
Protection for coal, for matches and knives;
Protection for hides, but none for our *wives*.

5.
Protection for tea, for coffee and spice;
Protection for rum, tobacco and vice;
Protection for beer, for brandy and gin;
Protection for dice, for gambling and sin.

6.
Protection *from* cranks and Chinamen too;
Protection *from* men with consciences true;
Protection for men who deal out the drink;
Protection *from* men who reason and think.

No. 3o.

What I Like.

Words by EDWARD CARSWELL.

Music by SILVER LAKE QUARTETTE.

1. Old par - ty pol - i - ti - cians; We've trust-ed you to do
2. The par - ty that we stand for, A ba - by you have styled;
3. You've ruled the roost so long, sirs, You think you own the ranch;

A work that must and shall be done, But now we say to you —
It may be; but, we tell you, it's A might-y health-y child!
Look out ! a cy-clone's com - ing, that Will hoist you root and branch;

You can - not be de - pend-ed on, Ex - cept it be to shirk.
It creeps no long - er on its knees, It now can walk a - lone;
A storm of in - dig - na - tion, and It's com - ing pret - ty soon,

You grab the loaves and fish-es, but You nev - er do the work.
It's put - ting on its mus-cle, and Its back's a sol - id bone.
With a shout for Home pro-tec-tion, and A - way with the sa - loon.

What I Like.—Concluded.

CHORUS.

I like an hon-est Dem-o-crat, Re-pub-li-can or Wump;

' But bless me if I like the chap Who dodg-es round the stump.

No. 37. The Prohibition Army.

Words by FRANK O. THURBER.　　　　　　Music by F. J. FULLER.

Recitive.

1. We are com-ing from the mountain, From the crys-tal stream and fount-ain,— Aft-er 'lec-tion do the count-in'— We're a
2. From.. snow-y Maine to Tex-as, Though whis-key rings may vex us, One un-bro-ken tie con-nects us, We're a
3. Though we fight a mon-ster e-vil 'Gainst the world, the flesh, the dev-il— If we all our heads keep lev-el We are

The Prohibition Army.—Concluded.

might-y ar-my corps. From the lake-side and the
pro-hi-bi-tion band. From Pa-cif-ic to At-
ver-y sure to win. See their strong-holds we have

riv-er, From the groves where sun-beams quiv-er, From the
lan-tic All the Rum-mies now are fran-tic, While old
ta-ken, See their forc-es sad-ly sha-ken, To de-

North where na-tions shiv-er, To the South-ern sun-ny shore.
par-ties are not an-tic,— Oh, there's trou-ble in the land.
struc-tion they'll a-wak-en Those sa-tan-ic sinks of sin.

4 Very plain 'tis, what we're doing,
Plain the pathway we're pursuing,
With a strength of Heaven's enduing
We shall surely win the day.
For so strong is our position
In the fort of Prohibition,
That already intuition
Makes us victors in the fray.

5 Though with license high we're haunted,
And the liquor flags are flaunted
In our faces; yet, undaunted
Stand we firmly in the fight;
Once again to save the nation,
Once again its real Salvation,
Pledging, without reservation,
All our forces for the right.

No. 38.

Conquering.

Allegro.

1. What, what, what, tho' small the cloud a-rose, O'er the
2. From, from, from its bo-som bless-ings pour, Join in

sky of hu-man woes; What tho' small, as hu-man hand,
large a-bun-dance show'r; Peace and love com-ming-ling flow,

Now it o-ver-spreads the land, Now it o-ver-spreads the land.
Temp'rance, thou art conq'ring woe, Temp'rance, thou art conq'ring woe.

3 Let, let, let your praise like incense rise,
   To the ruler of the skies;
   In his strength, to conquest go,
   ‖: Banish drink and human woe. :‖

4 Then, then, then his pow'r shall drunkards own,
   Sin's strong hold be overthrown;
   Man in man will find a friend,
   ‖: Joys begin that never end. :‖

From Temperance Melodeon, by permission.

69

No. 39.
Those Awful Cranks!

Words and Music by SILVER LAKE QUARTETTE.

1. These Cranks will be the death of us, If long they have their way;
2. We've done our best to hold them in, And check their on - ward course;

It fair - ly takes the breath of us, To hear them sing and pray.
And vain - ly sought to fold them in, By sweet, per - sua - sive force;

They stir the whole com-mu - ni - ty, With tell - ing speech and song;
We called them ev - 'ry name we could, And begged them to for - bear;

ritard.

And preach with cool im - pu - ni - ty, That we are go - ing wrong.
And piled on all the blame we could, But yet they do not care.

70

Those Awful Cranks!—Concluded.

Will be the death of us, Un-less we stop them quick;

They take the breath of us,

They make us faint and sick.

These Cranks

They take the breath of us,

3 Their tickets they will nominate,
Though ours may beaten go;
We never more can dominate
While they continue so.
We've done our best, unceasingly,
To break their growing ranks,
But yet they grow increasingly,
And smile at us with thanks.

4 The worst of all the trouble is,
We know that they are right;
Their number bound to double, is,
In every bitter fight.
We'd surely take a hand with them
Against the host of sin,
If certain that to band with them
The offices we'd win.

71

No. 40.   Uncle Sam is Waking Up.

Music by H. R. JEFFREY.

SOLO.   QUARTETTE.

1. See the peo - ple turn - ing out, What, what's the mat - ter?
2. Pro - hi - bi - tion is the cause, That's what's the mat - ter;

SOLO.   QUARTETTE.

What is all this noise a - bout? What, what's the mat - ter?
The peo - ple must have bet - ter laws, That's what's the mat - ter.

DUETT.

Gath-ered here from far and near, Men and wom-en all are here,
Laws that will our homes pro - tect, And the Sab - bath day re - spect,

QUARTETTE.

What is this the peo - ple fear? What, what's the mat - ter?
Tax and li - cense we re - ject, That's what's the mat - ter.

72

Uncle Sam is Waking Up.—Concluded.

CHORUS.

Cho. 1st verse. What, what's the mat - ter now? What, what's the mat - ter?
Cho. 2d, 3d, 4th verses. That's what's the mat - ter now, That's what's the mat - ter;

What's the mat - ter, tell us, now, What, what's the mat - ter?
Whis - key shops we won't al - low, That's what's the mat - ter.

3 Uncle Sam is waking up,
   That's what's the matter,
   From his snoozing o'er the cup,
   That's what's the matter.
   Some one heard the old man say:
   "Whiskey shops have had their day,
   You may pass the pledge this way,"
   That's what's the matter.

4 "Turn the keys on whiskey stills,
   That's what's the matter,
   Throw them into deepest wells,
   That's what's the matter.
   Close each brewery and saloon,
   Drunkard's will be sober soon,
   And will join and sing this tune,
   That's what's the matter."

73

No. 41.

Columbia's Men.

Words by T. B. Hawes.

Music by Silver Lake Quartette.

1. Co - lum - bia's hope is found-ed on the man - hood of her sons.
2. Your voice, cour-a - geous vo - ters; you have chil - dren, you have wives,

With gun - ners lack - ing cour - age, of what use are might - y guns!
Dare for - eign foe or trai - tor make at - tempt up - on their lives!

As use - less to a free - man is the bal - lot of the free,
Then speak! Do - mes - tic ruf - fians seek to trap them un - a - wares;

If cour - age does not will it for the right of lib - er - ty.
Speak out in voice like thun-der; say— "You shall not set the snares!"

Columbia's Men.—Concluded.

Not men, but sol-id man-hood, our coun-try needs, 'tis true;

Her need is now ap-peal-ing for that man-hood un-to you.

Then give it by your bal-lot in the bat-tle 'gainst the wrong,

Co-lum-bia must not per-ish, and the world must jog a-long.

3 Arouse, arouse, bold freemen! there are holy things at stake;
The women in the trenches will hold out till you awake.
Unarmed and unsupported, they are fighting with a will
For God and Home and Native Land, and you are sleeping still.

4 Reform! The day approaches. Let the breaking of the dawn
Find all the nation's patriots in solid column drawn.
Let Southern heart and Northern heart now consecrate our sod
To Unity and Liberty, to Purity and God.

75

No. 42.   Prohibition Rallying Song.

Words and Music by SILVER LAKE QUARTETTE.

1. Come, ye Chris-tian fa-thers, who've been pray-ing for the Right,
2. Come, ye man-ly broth-ers, who have sis-ters to pro-tect,

For God, and Home, and Na-tive Land, now make a gal-lant fight;
Ral-ly to the ranks of those, with homes blue rib-bon decked;

Stand for Pro-hi-bi-tion till the foe is put to flight,—
Swear that lives no more shall be by law's per-mis-sion wrecked, —

Sure-ly we're march-ing to vic-to-ry.
Sure-ly we're march-ing to vic-to-ry.

Prohibition Rallying Song.--Concluded.

CHORUS.

Hur-rah! hur-rah! we'll shout the ju - bi - lee; Hur-rah! hur-rah! from

rum we will be free; So we'll sing the cho - rus till the

foes of temp'rance flee,— Sure-ly we're marching to vic - to - ry.

3 Come, ye tipsy topers, from the bars that we would ban,
   Cease to paint your noses, on the danger signal plan ;
   Wear the temperance colors each, and vote to be a man, —
   Surely we're marching to victory.—CHORUS.

4 Don't you hear the word of cheer, go ringing down the lines?
   Don't you catch the music in the whisper of your pines?
   Listen to the echo from your busy marts and mines,—
   Surely we're marching to victory. —CHORUS.

The Good Time Coming.

(COMING RIGHT ALONG.)

HUTCHINSON FAMILY, by per.

Moderato.

1. Be - hold, the day of prom-ise comes, Full of in - spi - ra-tion,
2. Al - read - y in the gold - en east, The glo - ri - ous light is dawning,
3. And all the old dis - till - er - ies Shall per-ish and burn to - geth-er,

The bless-ed day, by proph-ets sung, For the heal-ing of the nations.
And watchmen from the mountain tops, Can see the bless - ed morning.
The Bran-dy, Rum, and Gin, and Beer, And all such, what - so - ev - er.

Old mid-night er - rors flee a - way; They soon will all be gone; While
O'er all the land their voic - es ring, While yet the world is napping, Till
The world be - gins to feel the fire, And e'en the poor be - sot-ter, To

heav'n-ly an - gels seem to say, "The good time's coming" on. O! the
e'en the sluggards be-gin to spring, As they hear the spir-its "rapping." O! the
save him-self from burning up, Jumps in the cool - ing wa-ter. O! the

CHORUS.

Good time, the good time, The good time's com - ing on; The

78

The Good Time Coming. Concluded.

good time, the good time, The good time's com - ing on.

Allegretto.

Com-ing right a - long, Com-ing right a - long, Ha! ha! ha! ha! ha!

Com-ing right a - long, Coming right a - long, Com-ing right a - long.

No. 44. The Prohibition Wagon.

Tune—WAIT FOR THE WAGON.

1 The good old party wagons in which we used to ride—
Republican and Democrat—must soon be thrown aside;
They've taken too much freight on board, and soon there'll be a break,
And anxiously we're asking, "What wagon shall we take?"

CHORUS—Hurrah for the wagon, the Prohibition wagon,
Wait for the wagon and we'll all take a ride!

2 They say it doesn't travel fast, but it is true and tried;
'Twont catch the offices just yet, but then we'll have the ride.
So let's hold on for principle with all our strength and might,
And just drive on straight forward, for we know the road is right.

3 The road is clear before us, and will not turn aside,
Till we drive up to the White House, and there we'll end our ride;
We'll rule this Yankee land awhile and banish the saloon,
So get on board if you will go, we start off very soon!

HEBERT WHITNEY.

79

No. 45.   The Breaking Clouds.

The Bells!

Words and Music by C. H. MEAD, by per.

The Bells!............ The Pro - hi - bi - tion Bells!

The Bells!...

The Bells!......................

What joy!

What joy!............ What joy their mu - sic tells!

What joy!...

What joy!......................

DUETT.

1. The clouds of wrong be - gin to break, We see the dawn - ing light;
2. Stand up, ye men, nor doubt nor fear, But brave - ly dare and do;
3. Ye loy - al men, stand at the polls, And let your votes go down;

While full and strong the bells ring in The bless - ed day of right.
Be true to God, and know that He Will sure be true to you.
The right shall win, and God him - self Will all right ef - forts crown.

86

The Breaking Clouds.—Concluded.

CHORUS.

Then work and pray, and vote a - way, Each loy-al ef - fort tells;

Keep working and praying, and vot-ing a - way,

With joy we'll sing, and glad - ly ring The Pro-hi - bi - tion Bells!

While joy-ous - ly sing-ing, and mer-ri - ly ringing,

No. 46. New Battle Hymn of the Republic.

*Tune—*JOHN BROWN.

1 We have lifted up our banner in a just and righteous cause,
We have set our faces forward and we will not idly pause
Till we've cleansed our land from evil and have purified our laws,
    For God is marching on,

CHORUS.—Glory, glory, hallelujah! Glory, glory, hallelujah!
    Glory, glory, hallelujah! Our God is marching on.

2 Never more in any measure will we touch the cursed thing,
It can only loss and sorrow to the State and people bring,
For it biteth like a serpent, like an adder's is its sting,
    But God is marching on.

3 He is marching on to battle, and he calleth not in vain,
That his chosen follow onward, for his hosts fill all the plain,
Where the last great cause is tested and the monster will be slain,
    For God is marching on.

4 The first dawning light is breaking, the full day we yet shall see,
When the cause of all our sorrow will be banished utterly,
And our homes be pure as heaven, and our sons be brave and free,
    For God is marching on.

81

HERBERT WHITNEY

No. 47.

Fortifying.

Words and Music by SILVER LAKE QUARTETTE.

1. O Blaine, of Maine, Has a new re-frain: "Our coast de-fens-es are
2. With-in may grin, In their work of sin, Dis-loy-al hosts that our
3. The State may wait For a bet-ter fate Than want and wretchedness,
4. Then whis-ky buy Till you drink and die; On Manhood's ru-in rear

far too risk-y;" Come, then, say I,— Let us for-ti-fy, And
Na-tion throt-tle; Feel no a-larm At their threats of harm,—We
crime and sor-row; We'll tax to-day What will sur-est pay,— No
mar-tial glo-ry! Each frown-ing fort Shall give loud re-port Of

bar all dan-ger with bars of whis-ky! If foes up-rose Where the
for-ti-fy with their keg and bot-tle! Though cries up-rise To the
statesman cares for the near to-mor-row! Yet Blaine, of Maine, With his
shame, disgrace, as the Na-tion's sto-ry! And swift up-lift, Thro' the

Gulf Stream flows, And hurled their mis-siles of dan-ger stead-y, How
lead-en skies, From child-hood, wom-an-hood, bruised and dy-ing,— We'll
new re-frain,—His coast de-fens-es, and tax on whis-ky, Would
a-zure's rift, Our Star-ry Flag, of our sin the to-ken, In

Fortifying.—Concluded.

should we stand For our Na-tive Land. If coast de-fens-es were
give no heed, But with state-ly greed We'll whis-ky tax for our
make you think That by tax-ing drink He'd save our land from a
shame un-furled To the scorn-ing world, While hearts bleed on, and our

CHORUS. Then whis-ky buy!.............
CHO. last verse. O men of might!

not all read-y?
for-ti-fy-ing!
mor-row risk-y!
homes are bro-ken!

CHORUS. We will for-ti-fy With
CHO. last verse. For the Truth and Right, Rise

Our coun-try calls...... ......
And pure and true ....

what you pay for the curse of cur-ses!
up, and swear from the shame to save us!

For her
All her

Rit.............

frown-ing walls. Though Man-hood starve with its emp-ty pur-ses!
bor-ders through This Land we'll keep that our fa-thers gave us!

83

No. 48. Who'll Kill dat Snake?

Words by F. A. WOODWARD.

Music by SILVER LAKE QUARTETTE.

SOLO

1. Oh, de whis - key snake, so... might - y bold, Dat it seem he..
2. He gob-ble de man and his farm right down, And seems like he
3. De Dem-o-crats built him a li - cense shed, For fear some

CHORUS.

nev - er would lose his hold.
wants ebery - ting in town. } Who'll kill dat snake? Prohi - bi-tion, Pro - hi -
crank hit him ou de head.

bi-tion. Who'll kill dat snake? Pro-hi - bi-tion, Pro-hi-bi-tion. Who'll kill dat

snake? Pro-hi - bi-tion kill him sure. (*Spoken by Bass*) Pro-hi - bi-tion, sure!
(Who'll kill dat snake?)

4 Republicans say, Prohibition will fail;
Take Local Option, whack him on de tail.

5 But de Prohibition gates are open wide,
Dey is open for you to come inside.

S-1

No. 49. The Temperance Banner.

Tune—STAR SPANGLED BANNER.

1 Oh, say, can you see by the dawn's early light
What so long we have hoped for with hearts sorely aching –
The swift flash of the sword that shall fall in its might,
The power of King Alcohol evermore breaking?
    Nay, the Wine-god's red glare
    And the drunkard's wild prayer
Give proof thro' the night that the curse is still there.

CHORUS—Oh, say, shall the banner of Temp'rance yet wave
    O'er the *whole* of the land of the free and the brave?

2 Now the Truth's dimly seen through the smoke of the fray,
Advancing unharmed where the dread foe reposes,
With a sling and a stone the huge giant she'll slay,
Though a demon-forged armor his body encloses.
    Oh, the people will shout
    When his life-blood ebbs out,
And his million of bond slaves will join in the rout.

CHORUS—And the banner of Temp'rance in triumph shall wave
    O'er the whole of this land of the free and the brave.

3 Then where'll be the band who so vauntingly boast
That the price of men's souls is their lawful possession?
They will join in the ranks of the Temperance host,
Ashamed of the traffic and glad of repression.
    Even now we can see
    What most surely will be—
Prohibition, the watchword from sea unto sea.

CHORUS—While the Temperance banner victorious shall wave
    O'er the *whole* of the land of the free and the brave.

4 Oh, thus be it ever when freemen shall stand
With their votes to repel the foul fiend's desolation!
Then shall women and children with uplifted hand
Praise the Power that has made us a Temperance nation.
    "Then conquer we must,
    For our cause it is just;
And this be our motto: 'In God is our trust.'"

CHORUS—And the Temperance banner in triumph shall wave
    O'er the whole of this land of the free and the brave.

By Miss MARY E. PARKER.

No. 50.
Rallying Song.

Words by A. J. MORRIS.   Music by SILVER LAKE QUARTETTE.

1. There's a mur - mur in the dis - tance, ev - ery hour it loud - er grows;
2. Long we've dal - lied with the temp - ter that our homes to ru - in brings,
3. As men who love our coun - try, we have need to stem the tide
4. We ne'er can o - ver - come the foe by com-pro-mis - es light;

From the sun - ny South it ech - oes, to the North's e - ter - nal snows;
We have reg - u - lat - ed, li - censed, and a thousand oth - er things,
That so long has swept our her - i - tage with e - vils far and wide;
But sim - ply say to him, we know that we are in the right.

And each pa - triot hears the sum-mons, and full well the truth he knows;
But he on - ly grows the bold - er,—to the wind our claim he flings;
But we'll ral - ly to the res - cue, stand-ing close - ly side by side;
With "God and Home" for watchword, we are sure to win the fight:

Chorus.

Our cause is marching on. Then ral-ly, ral-ly, ral-ly, ral-ly, ral - ly to the

Rallying Song.—Concluded.

polls; Then ral - ly, ral - ly, ral - ly, ral - ly, Ral - ly to the polls; Yes,
ral-ly, ral-ly, ral-ly, ral-ly, Ral-ly to the polls, And vote for truth and right.

No. 51.
Voting Song.

Tune—MARCHING THROUGH GEORGIA.

1 Come and gather round, my friends! we'll sing a temperance song,
  Sing it with a spirit that will start our cause along,
  Sing it as we soon shall sing it — fifty thousand strong,
    While we are voting for temperance.

CHORUS—Hurrah! hurrah! 'twill bring the Jubilee!
  Hurrah! hurrah! the vote will make us free!
  Soon we'll sing the chorus from the mountain to the sea,
    While we are voting for temperance.

2 We shouted for old parties till we almost split our throat;
  We've carried our petitions in, enough to sink a boat;
  We've preached and prayed and pleaded, and done everything but vote,
    But *now* we are voting for temperance.

3 We'll fight it out upon this line if't takes a hundred years;
  We've burnt the bridge behind us, and we've flung away our fears;
  We'll gain the battle inch by inch, you'll know it by our cheers,
    While we are voting for temperance.

HERBERT WHITNEY.

No. 52.
Temperance Doxology.

Praise God from whom all blessings flow,
Praise Him who heals the drunkard's woe;
Praise Him who leads the temperance host,
Praise Father, Son, and Holy Ghost.

87

INDEX.

PARADISE.

A Novel.

BY GEN. LLOYD S. BRYCE.

Paradise represents a Western locality to which all persons seeking a speedy and easy divorce resort. The story consists of a lively narrative of the experiences of a considerable number of persons in high life in New York and other places, who went there for that purpose.

"This is a very interesting romance, and one that the reader cannot abandon until he has read it through."—*Christian Leader*, Cincinnati, Ohio.

"A society novel of great originality."—*State Journal*, Lincoln, Neb.

"None of its readers can escape its fascinations after once commencing its perusal."—*City Press*, Belfast, Me.

"The story is very ingeniously woven together and is bright and witty."—*Daily News*, Galveston, Tex.

"It is pleasant reading and is not without a moral."—*True Witness*, Montreal, Canada.

"A good deal of clever and humorous writing—now and then a stroke that is even brilliant. The story is good in many ways."—*The Tribune*, New York.

"Col. Bryce has doubtless enjoyed writing this book, and the reader will enjoy it also. The smile which the first page will arouse will scarcely leave his face when he has finished the last page."—*The Tribune*, Detroit, Mich.

"It is a lively story on the subject of divorce, abounding in extravagance, humor and satire, and is written in a style always fluent."—*The Sun*, New York.

"The story has decided merit."—*Woman's Journal*, Boston.

"The story has all the snap of a good comedy and is skillfully told. The dialogue contains much humor and is epigrammatic in style and often brilliant. The book is an exceedingly entertaining one, and, at the same time, it conveys an excellent moral lesson."—*Toronto Mail*, Ontario.

12mo, paper. Price, 25 cents.